NEAR

Nine True Stories of a
Wonderful Discovery

Compiled by
Richard Bennett
& Martin Buckingham

THE BANNER OF TRUTH TRUST

THE BANNER OF TRUTH TRUST

Head Office
3 Murrayfield Road
Edinburgh, EH12 6EL
UK

North America Office
PO Box 621
Carlisle, PA 17013
USA

banneroftruth.org

These chapters first published in 1994
This format first published in 2021
© The Banner of Truth Trust 2021

*

ISBN 978 1 80040 222 5

*

Typeset in 10/13 Minion Pro at
The Banner of Truth Trust, Edinburgh

Printed in the UK by
Buchanan McPherson Ltd., Hamilton

Contents

1

Bob Bush:
Once a Jesuit, Now a Child of God

I began my Catholic journey in a little country town in northern California in the USA. The town was so small that we did not have Mass every Sunday, but a priest used to come once a month if he possibly could to hold Mass in a big public hall.

I have both an older and a younger brother. My father had been trained at the University of Santa Clara. As a result, my parents thought it would be a good idea for us to attend a Roman Catholic boarding school. The Jesuits ran the school, and I was a student there for four years. Academically, it was a very good school, but the only type of religion to which we were exposed was Roman Catholic theology and tradition, with no emphasis on the Bible.

Desire to Serve God and Mankind

As graduation approached, I considered what I should do with my life. I thought that becoming a Jesuit priest could be a good way to honour and serve God and help mankind; that was all I knew. At that time, even when I left high school, I had a longing and a hunger in my heart to meet God and to know him. In fact, once when I was a senior (fourth and final year) in high school, I remember going out to the football field and just kneeling there in the dark with my arms up to the sky. I cried out, saying, 'God, God, where are You?' I really had a hunger for God.

Jesuit Seminary

I entered the Jesuit Order in 1953 after graduation from high school. When I entered the Order, the first thing that happened was that I was told I had to keep all the rules and regulations, that to do so would be pleasing to God, and that is what he wanted for me. We were taught the motto, 'Keep the rule and the rule will keep you.'

We read a lot about the lives of the saints, and right from the beginning I was trained to look at them as models to follow, not realizing that they had become saints because they had served the Catholic Church. I did seminary studies for a total of thirteen years, taking course after course and studying one thing after another. It finally ended in a study of theology, culminating in ordination in 1966.

Hunger for God, but No Peace

I still had a hunger in my heart for God. I had not met the Lord yet and still did not have peace. In fact, at that time I used to smoke and I was very nervous. I would pace back and forth in my room puffing one cigarette after another because of my inner unrest.

I entered a postgraduate program in Rome thinking I would be on top of the mountain, but the hunger in my heart persisted. I even spoke to a priest who was in charge of missionaries to Africa, since I wanted to go there as a missionary. I was aware that if I went to Africa, however, the only thing I could do was to tell people about what I had learned about the Catholic doctrines and what the Catholic Church had to offer, even though it had not satisfied me. I did not see how it could satisfy them either.

I studied during the years of Vatican Council II (1962–65) and was ordained a year after it ended. The documents from Vatican Council II were coming out from Rome and I thought everything would change. It was a time of discovery. I thought I would get to the rock-bottom truth, and this would change the world. This idea was the force that drove me. But I was not aware of any changes, as the same Catholic doctrines from the Council of Trent were still in place. So, I did not go to Africa, but returned to California where God had a surprise in store for me.

Leading a Prayer Group

While at a retreat house where I said Mass, a lady asked me if I would lead a home prayer group in her home. I had never led a prayer meeting in my life and did not know how it worked, but I thought that as I had been trained for all those years, I should be qualified to do it and assented. It was held every Thursday from 10 a.m. until noon. A group of people would gather and read only the Bible, sing praises to the Lord, and pray for one another's needs. I was still smoking at that time. Early on the morning, when the prayer meeting was due to take place, I paced back and forth and thought, 'Oh, why did I say I was going to go there?' I had not been at all enthusiastic about going, but when noon came, I did not want to leave. The power of the biblical Word was beginning to touch my heart and life.

Surprised by God's Grace

The great surprise the Lord had in store for me happened in this way. One night we went to a retreat house with a group of people from the home prayer meeting. The speaker asked at the end of his address, 'Now if there is anyone here who is hungry for God and has not been touched by God and wants God to touch his life, then come forward and we will pray for you.' It happened that a lady called Sonia came up to me and asked, 'Would you please ask my husband Joe to go forward and get prayed for?' I told her, 'Sonia, I can not do that. That would not really be honest because I have not been prayed for myself, so how can I ask him to go forward?' Now I am about six feet four inches tall and she was a very short lady. I will never forget it; she looked me in the face and put her finger up to me and said, 'I think you need to get prayed for yourself.' I laughed and said, 'Yes, I do.' What she did not realize was that there was great hunger in my heart. After all the years of studying I had not met God. I read my Bible at the prayer meetings, but I still did not know the sovereign God of the Bible or myself as a lost sinner before Him. This was the moment I prayed that God would change me, so I went forward and they laid hands on me and prayed over me. It was not because of any works that either they or I did, but it was truly by God's grace that I was born again. Jesus became real; the Bible became real. He changed my life. To those who read this, He is real and life changing. 'Not by works of righteousness which we have done, but according to his mercy he saved us, by the washing of regeneration, and renewing of the Holy Ghost' (*Titus* 3:5).

Our Prayer Group, and Conviction

It was August 1970 when God's grace truly touched me. We started a prayer group in a high school and it grew so large we had to move to a gymnasium. Before long we had 800 to 1,000 people coming every Friday night. We were stressing praise and worshipping and glorifying God. Based in the gymnasium where there were no statues or any other such thing, we had one manual, the Bible.

I had a lot to learn. It took me many years to realize that I was compromising by staying in the Roman Catholic Church. Throughout all of those years, I continued to stress that salvation is only in the finished work of Jesus Christ on the cross and not in infant baptism; that there is only one source of authority, which is the Bible, the Word of God; and that there is no purgatory, but rather that when we die we either go to heaven or hell.

Here is where the conflict came. Seeing people depend upon such false and deceiving beliefs for their salvation was heart wrenching to me. I felt that maybe God could use me to change things in the Catholic Church. I even had prayer sessions with people who felt the same way. We prayed that God would change the Roman Catholic Church so that we could remain Catholics. But to remain Catholic, I now see, is to be living a compromised life.

I finally realized, after much conviction of the Holy Spirit, that not giving myself totally to him, one hundred per cent, was grieving my Lord, as I was sinning a sin of compromise. I also came to realize that the Roman Catholic Church could not change. If it did change, there would be no pope, rosary, purgatory, priests, mass, etcetera. After 17 years of brainwashing, my brain was washed and cleansed by the Holy Spirit. In a word, what was happening to me over this period is explained in Romans 12:1–2:

I beseech you therefore, brethren, by the mercies of God, that ye present your bodies a living sacrifice, holy, acceptable unto God, which is your reasonable service. And be not conformed to this world: but be ye transformed by the renewing of your mind, that ye may prove what is that good, and acceptable, and perfect, will of God.

Research in India

By this time I had met another priest who has since left the Church of Rome. He was preaching the same kind of thing, spending half of the year in India and half in the United States. Victor Affonso was also a Jesuit, and I told him I thought it would be wonderful to go to India and to do some missionary work there. We could research the dogma and doctrines of the Catholic Church.

I went to India in 1986 and spent six months there doing missionary work. We were also able to spend a month with a group of people researching Catholic dogma in the light of the Scriptures. We were determined to follow what the Bible said; if Catholic doctrines contradicted that, we would reject them.

We saw that Jesus said, 'Come unto me,' and that in the Gospels we are told to pray to our Father in Jesus' name, never to a saint or to Mary. The disciples did not pray to Stephen, who died very early in the Acts of the Apostles, or to James, who was killed very early. Why would they do that when they had the resurrected Jesus with them? He said, 'For where two or three are gathered together in my name, there am I in the midst of them' (*Matt.* 18:20) They prayed to Jesus; they prayed to the Father; they had the guidance of the Holy Spirit and obeyed the commandments of God.

In India we discovered that the Catholic catechism had changed the Ten Commandments from the way they were in the Bible. In the Roman Catholic catechism, the first commandment is as it is in Scripture. The second commandment in the catechism is, 'Thou shalt not take the name of the LORD thy God in vain.' This is a complete change from the Bible. The third commandment of the Bible has been moved up to the second. The original second commandment as is found in Scripture has been dropped. Virtually all of the Roman Catholic catechisms drop the second commandment of the Bible. For example, the *New Baltimore Catechism,* Question 195, answers, 'The commandments of God are these ten: (1) I am the Lord thy God, thou shalt not have strange gods before me; (2) Thou shalt not take the name of the Lord thy God in vain,' etc. In the Bible, the second commandment is,

> Thou shalt not make unto thee any graven image, or any likeness of any thing that is in heaven above, or that is in the earth beneath, or that is in the water under the earth: Thou shalt not bow down thyself to them, nor serve them: for I the LORD thy God am a jealous God, visiting the iniquity of the fathers upon the children unto the third and fourth generation of them that hate me; And shewing mercy unto thousands of them that love me, and keep my commandments (*Exod.* 20:4–6).

God forbids us to bow down before these or to serve them, yet there are pictures of the pope bowing down and kissing statues.

We were bothered that this commandment had been dropped out of the catechism. So now we might well ask, 'How do we get ten commandments?' What the catechisms do is divide the last commandment (formerly the tenth, now split into the ninth and tenth). 'Do not covet thy neighbour's wife' is listed as a separate commandment from that of not coveting his goods. This is quite a distortion of the Bible. I was discovering dogmas and doctrines that directly contradicted the Scriptures.

Mary and the Mass

We also investigated the doctrine of the Immaculate Conception. This is defined as 'the doctrine that Mary was conceived without sin; at the first moment of conception there was no sin there'. This contradicts Romans 3:23 which says, 'For all have sinned and come short of the glory of God.' Here we had a doctrine, a tradition that is passed down and solemnly defined as infallibly true, and it contradicts what is in the Bible.

Then we came to one of the biggest areas of conflict. It had to do with the sacrifice of the Mass. The official Catholic position on the sacrifice of the Mass is that it is a continuation of the sacrifice of Calvary. The Council of Trent actually defined it this way:

> And since in this divine sacrifice, which is celebrated in the Mass, that same Christ is contained and immolated in an unbloody manner, who on the altar of the cross 'once offered Himself' in a bloody manner (*Heb.* 9:27), the holy Synod teaches that this is truly propitiatory . . . For it is one and the same victim, the same one now offering by the ministry of the priests as He who then offered Himself on the Cross, the manner of offering alone being different . . .

Some people might say the Council of Trent is not valid any more and that things have changed. But Cardinal Ratzinger [now Pope Emeritus Benedict XVI], then head of the Congregation for the Doctrine of the Faith (which is the old Holy Office), in a book called *The Ratzinger Report*, said, 'It is likewise impossible to decide in favour of Trent and Vatican I, but against Vatican II. Whoever denies Vatican II denies the authority that upholds the other two councils and thereby detaches them from their foundation.' Catechisms say the same thing, that the Mass is the same sacrifice as that of the cross. For example, the *New Baltimore Catechism* says, 'The Mass is the same sacrifice as the sacrifice of the cross because in the Mass the victim is the same, and the principal priest is the same, Jesus Christ.' Yet in Hebrews 10:18 it says, 'Now where remission of these is, there is no more offering for sin.' So Scripture makes it very clear. In fact, eight times in four chapters, beginning in chapter seven of the letter to the Hebrews, it says 'once for all'; there was one offering for sin, once for all!

A Finished Sacrifice

Anyone who has attended Mass in the Catholic Church will remember the prayer said by the priest, 'Pray, brethren, that our sacrifice may be acceptable to God, the Almighty Father.' This is a very serious prayer. The people respond saying the same thing, asking that the sacrifice may be acceptable to God. But this is contrary to the Word of God because the sacrifice has already been accepted. When Jesus was on the cross, he said, 'It is finished' (*John* 19:30) and we know that it was completed because Jesus was accepted by the Father and rose from the dead and is now at the right hand of the Father. The Good News that we preach is that Jesus has risen from the dead, that his sacrifice is completed, and that he has paid for sin. When by God's grace we accept his work as the finished sacrifice for our sins, we are saved and have everlasting life.

A memorial is a remembrance of something that someone has done for us. Jesus said, 'This do in remembrance of me' (*Luke* 22:19). So, anyone reading this, or any priest who is saying Mass, must seriously consider the error of the prayer, 'Let us pray, my brothers and sisters, that our sacrifice may be acceptable.' The sacrifice has been accepted and it is done. We are to have the communion service in memory of what Jesus has done. We see that the sacrifice that Jesus offered on the cross was sufficient and final. It cannot be added to or re-enacted.

Can the Mass Atone for Sin?

The Catholic Church says that the Mass is a propitiatory sacrifice effective to take away the sins of those on earth and those who have died. That is why, to this very day, even though some people will say that the Church in some places does not believe in purgatory, still virtually every Mass that is said is for someone who has died. It is believed that the Mass will shorten their time in purgatory. That is why it is said for dead people. When a person dies, judgment immediately follows, 'It is appointed unto men once to die, but after this the judgment' (*Heb.* 9:27). If they are saved, they go directly to heaven; if they remain in their sins, they go to hell. There is nothing to change one from hell to heaven. Yet the Catholic Church believes that the Mass, being a propitiatory sacrifice, will decrease the time in purgatory. But all the suffering and all the atonement that was ever made for sins was accomplished by Jesus on the cross, and we need to accept this truth. We need to receive everlasting life and to be born again while we are still alive. There is no biblical evidence to support the idea that after death we can experience any kind of change.

To Be Right before God

We then began to study what the Roman Catholic Church teaches on salvation. It is a doctrine of the Church that we can be saved by being baptized as infants. Present-day canon law says, 'Baptism, the gate to the sacraments, necessary for salvation, in fact, or at least in intention, by which men and women are freed from their sins, reborn as children of God, configured to Christ . . .' (Canon 849). This means that when a baby is baptized, it is saved and has everlasting life by virtue of baptism. But that is not true. Jesus never said anything like that, neither is there a word in the Bible about anything like that happening. There is no limbo! Jesus said, 'Suffer the little children to come unto me.' The Bible always says we are saved when we accept that Christ Jesus totally paid the price of our sin so that his right standing with God becomes ours. 'For he hath made him to be sin for us, who knew no sin; that we might be made the righteousness of God in him' (2 *Cor.* 5:21).

Christ's Work or Our Works?

The Roman Catholic Church then goes on to say that in order to be saved one must keep its laws, rules, and regulations. And if these laws are violated (for example, laws concerning birth control or fasting or attendance at Mass every Sunday), then you have committed a sin. The Church says in canon law of the present day that if you commit a serious sin, that sin must be forgiven by confessing it to a priest. 'Individual and integral confession and absolution constitute the only ordinary way by which the faithful person who is aware of serious sin can be reconciled with God, and with the Church' (Canon 9609).

The Church says that this is the way sins are forgiven, the ordinary way that sins are forgiven. The Bible says that if we repent from the heart and believe on Christ's finished sacrifice we are saved. We are saved by grace, not by our works. The Roman Catholic Church adds works, in that you have to do these specific things in order to be saved, whereas the Bible says in Ephesians 2:8–9 that it is by grace that we are saved, not by works. The Bible makes it very clear that we are saved by grace. It is a free gift from God, not because of any works we do. 'For by grace are ye saved through faith; and that not of yourselves; it is the gift of God; not of works, lest any man should boast' (*Eph.* 2:8–9). 'And if by grace then is it no more of works; otherwise grace is no more grace. But if it be of works, then is it no more grace; otherwise work is no more work' (*Rom.* 11:6).

I Leave India and Roman Catholicism

We examined these and many other doctrines while we were in India, and as I left, I knew that I could not represent the Roman Church any longer. I began to see that Roman Catholic dogmas, which contradict Scripture, are so rooted that they cannot be changed.

The Catholic charismatic movement today has gone back to these fundamental dogmas and doctrines of Rome. It maintains and holds on to these, and so that whole movement has been totally undermined. The Catholic charismatic movement is not a fresh breath of air blowing through the church, changing everything by moving it back to the Bible. Everything cannot get back to the Bible because the Roman Catholic Church will not let it go back that far. The Roman Catholic Church is not going to let go of the Mass and let it be a memorial as Jesus said. It will always insist that the Mass is an ongoing continuation of the sacrifice of Jesus. The Roman Catholic Church will not let go of the dogma that babies are reborn and receive eternal life at baptism, even though this was not taught in the early church. This teaching did not begin until the third century, and was not universal until the fifth century. The Roman Catholic Church is not going to let go of this or of any of the other requirements that are put upon their people.

Now I do sincerely love Roman Catholics and want to help them. I want to help them find the freedom of salvation and the life and blessing that comes from following the Scriptures. And I have nothing against any Catholic or any priest; it is the dogmas and doctrines that keep them bound. In chapter seven of Mark, Jesus said, 'For laying aside the commandments of God, ye hold the tradition of men' (*Mark* 7:8). That is the problem we are facing here. These traditions destroy the very Word of God because they contradict its truths.

When I left India and came home, I knew that I was facing the biggest change of my life. It was a time of great distress for me because I had really totally believed in the Roman Catholic Church and had served it for so much of my life. I knew when I came back I was going to have to leave the Church of Rome.

In 1987, I left the Catholic Church formally by writing a letter of resignation and then corresponding back and forth with my former superiors, because I wanted to witness to all of them. I ended up writing to Rome before I left. I did it in that manner because I wanted to witness to all of them and give them reasons why I was leaving. I wanted to follow the Bible. .

My Parents and My Wife

When I returned from India, I was experiencing a great deal of suffering. I came home to my parents, both of whom were over eighty, and one night we had a serious conversation. I told them what I was going to do; I told them that I was saved by God's grace and I was going to leave the Roman Church for doctrinal reasons. There was a big pause and then my father said, speaking very slowly, 'Bob, you know, both your mother and I have been thinking the same thing.' They went to one more Mass and came home and said, 'Do you know that is an altar in the front of the church? An altar is a place of sacrifice.' And my father said, 'I see clearly now there is no more sacrifice.' Both my parents began reading the Bible and following it. In 1989, my mother died while reading the Word of God and with the peace and assurance that she had everlasting life and was going to be with the Lord forever. My dad passed away in 1993 with a prayer on his lips for those he left behind. He had written his own testimony to the grace of God and, though quite old, he had witnessed to others, even in the retirement home.

On 6 June 1992, God gave me the greatest gift he can give a man besides salvation, my beautiful wife, Joan.

The Present Day

I am now an ordained minister, in fellowship with others of the biblical faith and continue to preach the gospel of God's grace, through the death of the Lord Jesus Christ alone.

2

Joseph Tremblay:
A Priest, but a Stranger to God

I was born in Quebec, Canada, in 1924. From childhood my parents inculcated in me a great respect for God. I desired intensely to serve him to the best of my ability and to consecrate myself totally to him in order to please him, according to the words of the apostle Paul: 'I beseech you therefore, brethren, by the mercies of God, that ye present your bodies a living sacrifice, holy, acceptable unto God, which is your reasonable service' (*Rom.* 12:1) It was the desire to please him that motivated my decision to take the Holy Orders of the Roman Catholic Church.

A Missionary to Bolivia

After several years of study, I was ordained a priest in Rome. One year later I was sent as a missionary to Bolivia and Chile, where I served for more than 13 years. I liked the life very much and tried to discharge my responsibilities as best I could. I enjoyed the friendship of all my co-workers, and even if they looked with a certain irony upon my pronounced taste for the study of the Bible, their invitations to share with them the results of my studies evidenced their approval. When they called me 'Joe the Bible', I knew that in spite of the sarcasm expressed, they envied me. My parishioners also appreciated the ministry of the Word of God, so much so that they organized a club for home Bible studies. I was compelled to give myself to earnest study of the Bible, as much to prepare myself for the improvised home meetings as to prepare my Sunday sermons.

Serious Bible Study

The study of the Bible, which until that time had been just a hobby, quickly became a professional obligation. I became aware of the clarity with which certain truths were taught, and, on the other hand, I discovered that nothing at all was written about many dogmas that I had studied. My study revealed that I did not know the Bible. I suggested to my superiors that I might go for further studies in the Bible when my turn for vacation arrived. In the meantime, the Jesuits at Antofagasta invited me to teach the Bible at the Normal School of the University, which they directed. I do not know how they learned of my interest in the Bible. Notwithstanding my lack of preparation, I accepted the invitation, knowing that this new responsibility would necessitate even more serious study of the Word of God.

The Gospel Via Radio

How many hours, days, and nights were consecrated to the preparation of my classes, my meetings, and my sermons! To maintain a good morale during my readings and studies, I had the habit of listening to music. I had been given a little transistor radio on which I could listen to beautiful background music without the bother of changing records. It was thus that one day I became aware that it was religious songs and hymns that were coming through to me on the little radio. I heard the word 'Jesus' from time to time while I was reading the Bible or commentaries.

The atmosphere was very propitious. But the hymns did not last long. A short Bible reading followed them. The last verse that was read caught my attention: 'For he hath made him to be sin for us, who knew no sin; that we might be made the righteousness of God in him' (2 *Cor.* 5:21). The sermon that followed was based on this verse. At first I was tempted to change the station, because it was too distracting to listen to someone speaking while trying to study. In addition, I thought to myself: What could this ministry add to me, after all, me with all my degrees? I could teach him a thing or two. After a moment's hesitation I decided to listen to what the speaker had to say, and, truly, I learned some of the most wonderful things concerning the Person of Jesus Christ. I was even filled with shame, knowing without a doubt that I could not have done as well as the one who had preached.

It had seemed to me that it was Jesus himself who had been speaking to me, who was there before me. And how little I knew him, this Jesus, who, nevertheless, was the subject of my thoughts, and of my studies. I felt that he was far from me. It was the first time that such a feeling concerning Jesus Christ had ever presented itself to me. He seemed to be a stranger. It was as if all of my being were but emptiness, around which I had erected a structure of principles and theological dogmas, very beautiful, well-constructed, well-illustrated, but which had not touched my soul, which had not changed my being. I felt as if there were a great emptiness in me. And in spite of the fact that I continued to study and to gorge myself with reading, praying, and meditating, this emptiness became even greater with each day that passed.

I Learn Salvation by Grace

I went on listening to this same radio station, tuning in to every programme that I could. I learned that the station was HCJB in Quito,

Ecuador. I learned also that it was a radio station consecrated exclusively to preaching the gospel to the whole world. Sometimes I was very much touched by all that I heard, and on such occasions I wrote directly to the station to thank them and to ask for information. What struck me most in all that I heard was the insistence with which they spoke of salvation by grace: that all the credit for the salvation of man was given, not to the one who was saved, but to the Lord Jesus Christ, the only Saviour; that man could boast of nothing, that his works were but filthy rags, that eternal life could be received within the heart only as a free gift, that it was not a reward in exchange for merits that had been acquired but was an unmerited gift given by God to whosoever repents of his sins and receives Jesus Christ into his heart and life as personal Saviour. All of this was new to me. It was contrary to the theology I had been taught: that heaven and eternal life are gained by means of one's merit, faithfulness, charity, and sacrifices. And this is what I had been working at for so many years. But what was the result of my efforts?

As I considered this question I said to myself, 'I'm no further forward. If I commit a mortal sin, I'll go to hell if I die in that state. My theology has taught me that salvation is by works and sacrifices. I discover in the Bible a free salvation. My theology gives me no assurance of salvation; the Bible offers me that assurance. I'm confused. Perhaps I should stop listening to those Evangelical programmes.'

My inner battle was taking on alarming proportions. I suffered in my body and in my heart, with headaches, insomnia, and fear of hell. I had no desire to celebrate Mass or listen to confessions. My soul had greater need of pardon and consolation than all the other souls with which I was in contact. I avoided everybody.

But God continued to speak to me in the solitude of my anguished heart. So many questions came up in my spirit; so many misgivings smouldered in my heart. The Word of God came to my rescue, spreading a refreshing balm upon my fevered emotions. 'For God so loved the world, that he gave his only-begotten Son, that whosoever believeth in him should not perish, but have everlasting life' (*John* 3:16). 'For all have sinned, and come short of the glory of God; Being justified freely by his grace through the redemption that is in Christ Jesus' (*Rom.* 3:23–24). 'For the wages of sin is death; but the gift of God is eternal life through Jesus Christ our Lord' (*Rom.* 6:23). Many other texts came to mind, texts that I now knew because I had heard them often on the radio over station HCJB.

Holy Mother Church

I decided to talk to my superior. A very wise man and a real father to everyone, he had already noticed my attitude. I had changed, he commented; something was wrong. I told him why I had changed. He let me talk. In concluding my confession I said to him: 'I would like not only to read and study the Bible, but also to try to adapt my life to it, to live according to what is written in it without impositions of men.' The reply was very vague. He didn't want to offend me. He counselled me to continue reading the Bible, but reminded me that I must maintain my faithfulness to the teachings of our 'mother, the holy church', to whom one must submit even in the things one does not understand. I listened to my superior with all the respect that I owed him. He was not himself sure of his salvation. But in my heart I had lost faith in my church because it didn't teach the assurance of salvation. A crack had begun to open in my heart which was going to grow larger and break everything, and that quicker than I thought. The light dawned in my heart at the moment that I least expected it. It was my turn to preach in my parish. For that Sunday I had chosen as my theme, 'Religious Hypocrisy', and availed myself of the Bible text: 'Not every one that saith unto me, Lord, Lord, shall enter into the kingdom of heaven; but he that doeth the will of my Father which is in heaven. Many will say to me in that day, Lord, Lord, have we not prophesied in thy name? and in thy name have cast out devils? and in thy name done many wonderful works? And then will I profess unto them, I never knew you: depart from me, ye that work iniquity' (*Matt.* 7:21–23).

The Holy Spirit Works

I knew my parishioners; I wanted to draw their attention to the vainglory manifested by certain persons with respect to their good works, forgetting that very often these good works camouflaged a corrupt heart. As I delivered my message, I was conscious that the Word of God was coming back to me, as a ping-pong ball that flies back and hits the player in the face. It is curious to see how the human spirit, in just a few seconds, can construct a complete framework of thought, which would perhaps require hours to be put into words. It was thus that, while I was giving my message, someone else was speaking in my heart and preaching a sermon to me that was precisely adapted to my personal needs. I thought that, because I was religious and a priest, I was better than all those who were listening to me. And yet, to me also, this word would resound one day in my ears: 'I never knew you: depart from me.'

I heard my own arguments in the face of this threat and this condemnation: 'How is it possible, my God, that you will not know me? Am I not your priest? Am I not religious? Look at all the sacrifices I have made for you: the years of study, the separation from my parents and my country, my vows of poverty, obedience, and chastity, consecrating to you all my riches, my will, my body even, in order to better serve you. And you will say to me that you never knew me? Consider all the sufferings that I have endured during my missionary life: I have not always eaten to my fill, I have cried with those who cried, I have baptized children by the hundreds, I have listened to all sorts of confessions, I have comforted so many tearful, discouraged souls, I have suffered cold, loneliness, contempt, ingratitude, threats . . . I am ready even to give my life for you.' But in spite of all the arguments that I presented to God, the same condemnation continued to ring in my ears: 'I never knew you.' I was at the end of arguments, at the end of my strength. I felt as if I were going to break down and cry right there before the parishioners, who also sensed the approaching storm. And then the storm broke. The tears prevented me from continuing my sermon. The discouragement when confronted with this terrible frustration of my whole life purpose, in face of my sins and the condemnation of God, was too much for me to bear. I took refuge in my office.

There, on my knees, I waited until calm returned. Where could I turn now? Perhaps my theology would save me, if I returned to it and faithfully followed all its dogmas and precepts. But that theology to which I considered attaching myself once again had already begun to experience disorder, change, destruction. My thoughts turned to my friends. But they were in the same situation as I: uncertain. Trust in myself? I could no longer count on my good works. To look at me, I was a total wreck. I could do no more; I was in a state of complete exhaustion, depressed and discouraged. This was God's moment to give me his grace. 'Man's extremity is God's opportunity.'

After Conviction – The Answer

During all my reflections, God was preparing his word of salvation: 'For by grace are ye saved through faith; and that not of yourselves: it is the gift of God: Not of works, lest any man should boast' (*Eph.* 2:8–9). It was here that I understood my error and the reason for God's rejection. I had been trying to save myself by my works; God wanted to save me by grace. Someone else had already taken care of my sins and of the judgment attached to them. This someone was Jesus Christ. It was for this that he died on the cross. It was for the sins of another that he died, for he himself had never sinned. For whose sins, then, did he die? Could it be mine? Yes, mine. I remembered the words of Jesus: 'Come unto me, all ye that labour and are heavy laden, and I will give you rest' (*Matt.* 11:28). I understood that I must go to Jesus if I wanted to have the assurance of salvation and peace of soul. I intended to ask him: 'But where are you, Jesus, so that I might cling to you?' But even before this cry of impatience arose in my heart, the Lord comforted my heart through his Word.

Now I knew where Jesus was. He was closer than I had thought. And I hurried to invite him to enter into my heart, without taking the time to ask permission of any man. 'Come in, Lord Jesus; come into my heart. Be its Leader, its Master, O Beloved Saviour.' At that moment I knew that I was freed from the punishment that had menaced me for such a long time. I was saved—pardoned. I had eternal life. God had begun his work in me. Now I understood the words that I had heard so often and which had become real to me: 'For he hath made him to be sin for us, who knew no sin; that we might be made the righteousness of God in him' (2 Cor. 5:21). 'But he was wounded for our transgressions, he was bruised for our iniquities: the chastisement of our peace was upon him; and with his stripes we are healed' (Isa. 53:5).

My Struggle to Continue

What happened after that? At first I continued my priestly service as best I could. But little by little I began to feel like a stranger in that position. I realized that the grace that had saved me, that had made of me a child of God, was going to enter into conflict with the 'works' of the position in which I was trying to live. I was happy because I had the assurance of my salvation. But I was stifled in a setting in which I was pushed to do good works in order to merit my salvation. Salvation, I had; therefore, all of these works began to be put aside, one after the other. The orientation and presentation of my preaching changed. All that interested me was Jesus Christ: who he was and what he had done.

I abandoned the subjects prepared in advance by the liturgical organization of the diocese, in order to devote all of my efforts to the Person and work of my beloved Saviour, presenting him as such to my bewildered parishioners, confused but often edified. I asked to be released from my functions as a parish priest, since I could no longer preach that which contradicted the Word of God. My superiors accepted my resignation, though they could not understand why I wanted to leave. They had, in fact, treated me very well, indulged me in many ways; as far as they were concerned, I lacked nothing. This was true, as far as food, clothing, housing, etc., were concerned. But now I had the assurance of my salvation. Christ was now my Master. I had nothing more to do to gain my salvation; it had been gained by Another. He would therefore take it upon himself to continue the work begun, since he never does his work by halves.

Christians Visit Me

I returned to Quebec, Canada, in 1965, for an extended period of rest. Shortly after, Evangelical Christians visited me. How did they know of my interest in the Word of God? They were frank with me: the personnel of HCJB radio station had given my name to them. However, even if I found their conversation very edifying, I did not give myself wholly to them. I did not want to fall into another theological system, having been oppressed for years by the system into which I had been born and in which I had grown up and lived during some forty years. Nevertheless, I prayed to the Lord to find for me brothers and sisters to whom I could join myself, so that I would not feel so alone.

I knew the experience of the first Christians, according to the report given in Acts, 'And they continued steadfastly in the apostles' doctrine and fellowship, and in breaking of bread, and in prayers' (*Acts* 2:42). Was it possible that Christians still met together in our day in order to remember the Lord, while awaiting His return? God, who had provided for the salvation of my soul, would provide again, in order to disclose to me the existence of his children.

New Duty

My superiors in Montreal called me one day to invite me to replace a Professor of Theology in a College in Rouyn. I hesitated about accepting the position, principally because I had never liked the Abitibi region, of which Rouyn is the main city. However, I accepted, since it would be only for a few months. The subject I was given to teach was 'The Church'. I was given access to all of the books that would be necessary for the preparation of my classes.

I began my preparations using only the Bible. I explained to the students what the church is, according to the Bible. I admit that I had difficulty myself in understanding what I was teaching. It was such a contrast to the hierarchical church in which I still found myself. I very much enjoyed the study of this subject. I used a little tape recorder to illustrate the lessons, playing for the students certain interviews that I held with the general public in different places of the city.

One day I learned from the newspaper that a television programme was to be presented having as its subject: 'The Church'. I recorded the programme in order to use it in my classes and discovered that the subject was treated from the point of view of what the Bible taught. I was so impressed by the similarity between the presentation by this unknown person, whom I later learned was an Evangelical Christian, and my own, that I sent a note of thanks to the preacher, inviting him to come to see me, if this were possible. He came, and I recognized in him someone who knew the Lord. After several visits, he invited me to his home to spend Sunday with him and his family. On the occasion of that visit, I attended a 'Remembrance of the Lord' service for the first time.

God Answers Prayer

I recognized in this service that which was described in 1 Corinthians 11 and realized that God had answered my prayer, having led me to my brothers and sisters in the Lord, and having shown me that Christians in our day do indeed meet together as a local church to remember the Lord while awaiting His return. 'For as often as ye eat this bread, and drink this cup, ye do shew the Lord's death till he come' (*1 Cor.* 11:26).

Shortly after, I wrote my superiors in Montreal, announcing to them the news that I had found my family and requesting that they obtain for me a dispensation from all the vows I had made to the Roman Catholic Church, since I no longer considered myself a member. My life now belonged to the Lord and its direction was henceforth under his control.

New Life in the Lord

It was thus that the Lord liberated me, not only from my sins, not only from his condemnation, but also from every system of man, which burdens and suppresses. 'There is therefore now no condemnation to them which are in Christ Jesus, who walk not after the flesh, but after the Spirit. For the law of the Spirit of life in Christ Jesus hath made me free from the law of sin and death' (*Rom.* 8:1–2).

3

Alexander Carson:
Free Indeed

From childhood to age forty-four, seventeen years as a Roman priest (1955–72), the Roman Catholic Church had been the pillar of truth to me, and my infallible guide to God. This pillar of truth was not constructed solely of the infallible Scriptures, but also constructed of man's traditions apart from Scripture, which were held to be revelations from God, but which in fact contradicted, and were in opposition to the plain teachings of Scripture.

During the first century AD, in the days of the Apostles, truth was being preached in the streets and Temple areas of Jerusalem. *Acts* 6:7 bears testimony to that preaching: 'And the word of God increased; and the number of the disciples multiplied in Jerusalem greatly; and a great company of the priests were obedient to the faith.' At great personal cost, those Jewish Old Testament priests left all they had to follow Jesus. When their hearts were pierced by the truth, that 'two-edged sword', the Word of God (*Heb.* 4:12), they left all to follow Jesus. All former Catholic priests who have become 'obedient to the faith' can certainly relate to this passage in Acts, from Wyclif, Hus, and Luther, down to the present day. At different times and in various ways God has used his written Word to set men, even Catholic priests, free! 'Then said Jesus to those Jews which believed on him, If ye continue in my word, then are ye my disciples indeed; And ye shall know the truth, and the truth shall make you free' (*John* 8:31–32). In 1972, while I was pastor of Sacred Heart Catholic Church, Rayville, Louisiana, U.S.A., the Lord's truth and grace became as clear as day to me. Here is my full story.

Baptism, First Communion, and Confirmation

In 1928, I was baptized into the Roman Catholic Church as an infant. When I was just over a year old my family moved from New York State to New Milford, Connecticut, where I was raised in the Catholic faith. I thoroughly believed in all Catholic practices and beliefs, and I took my relationship to the Church, and therefore to God, very seriously. My first communion and confirmation were important events to me. After high school, I went to Tufts College in Boston for pre-medical studies, hoping one day to become a medical doctor like my revered uncle. However, at the end of two years of study, I really desired to become a priest. I felt it was more important to help people spiritually than to aid them medically.

The Seminary

In September 1948 I began studies for the priesthood at St John's Seminary in Brighton, Massachusetts. How I loved the seminary! Everything was so 'holy' there. Nevertheless, at the end of my first year in the seminary, I withdrew. I felt I could never measure up to being a priest, being convinced at the time that it was the highest possible call on a young man's life. I attended Boston College (Jesuit) and served Mass almost every morning at a local Catholic monastery. At this time, during the autumn of 1949, God saved me by his grace (the only way!) even though I did not know a lot about the Bible. Jesus saves the believing sinners even though they walk in a measure of confusion and darkness. I had come to a place where I was uncertain about my relationship with God, and I wanted to be sure about that above everything else.

A Confession Absolutely Different

One night I knelt in a confessional booth and confessed every sin of my life that I could bring to mind. At confession I always confessed my sins to God first, though it was in the presence of the priest who would give 'absolution'. 'If we confess our sins, he is faithful and just to forgive us our sins, and to cleanse us from all unrighteousness ...' (*1 John* 1:9). After I expressed my repentance, and while the priest was giving the ritual 'absolution', I cried out to God with my heart, saying, 'God, if you will forgive all my sins, I take you as Lord of my heart and I will serve you the rest of my life!' 'For whosoever shall call upon the name of the Lord shall be saved' (*Rom.* 10:13). Leaving that confessional box and walking across the transept of the church, I felt a great peace and 'Abba, Father!' rang in my heart. I knew that I had a right relationship with God! This did not happen because of the presence of a priest and liturgical absolution. It happened because of the presence of Jesus Christ, our great High Priest, who made intercession for me and who made me the object of his grace, mercy, and compassion. 'In whom we have redemption through his blood, the forgiveness of sins, according to the riches of his grace ... for by grace are ye saved through faith; and that not of yourselves: it is the gift of God: not of works, lest any man should boast' (*Eph.* 1:7, 2:8–9).

The next year, I re-entered the seminary to complete studies for the priesthood, the best way I knew to serve God at the time. I was ordained by Bishop Lawrence Shehan of Bridgeport, Connecticut, on 2 February 1955, and began ministry as a Diocesan, or secular priest, in the Diocese of Alexandria, Louisiana. The great excitement and joy I felt about my unique position of service began to wane after a few years, and try as I might to do everything right, it became empty, meaningless ritual.

The Bible – a New Standard

In 1971, after several years of crying out to God for something more meaningful, my great hunger was abated. Jesus and the Word of God (the Scriptures) became very real to me. Because 'the love of God is shed abroad in our hearts' (*Rom.* 5:5), the Holy Spirit led me to judge Roman Catholic theology by the standard of the Bible. Before, I had always judged the Bible by Catholic doctrine and theology. It was a reversal of authority in my life.

On a Sunday night in July 1972, I began to read the Book of Hebrews in the New Testament. This letter exalts Jesus, his priesthood, and his sacrifice over everything in the Old Covenant or Testament. This is some of what I read: 'Who needeth not daily, as those high priests, to offer up sacrifice, first for his own sins, and then for the people's: for this he did once, when he offered up himself' (*Heb.* 7:27). This startled me, and I began to feel very uneasy. I understood for the first time that Jesus' sacrifice was a one-time sacrificial offering at Calvary, in itself effectual to reconcile me to God, as well as believing penitents of all ages. I saw at this time that the 'Holy Sacrifice of the Mass' offered by me and thousands of other Catholic priests daily throughout the world was a fallacy and completely irrelevant. If the 'sacrifice' I daily offered as a priest was meaningless, then my 'Priesthood' which existed for the purpose of offering that 'sacrifice' was likewise without meaning. These realizations were soon clearly confirmed as I continued to read in Hebrews Chapter 10: 'But this man [Jesus], after he had offered one sacrifice for sins for ever, sat down on the right hand of God; from henceforth expecting till his enemies be made his footstool. For by one offering he hath perfected for ever them that are sanctified' (*Heb.* 10:12–14). 'Now where remission of these is, there is no more offering for sin' (*Heb.* 10:18).

Saved by God's Grace Alone

That night the Roman Catholic Church lost credibility for me, as it had taught as truth what was clearly contrary to the Scriptures. I then chose the Scriptures as my standard of truth, no longer accepting the *magisterium*, or teaching authority of the Catholic Church as my standard. In my letter of resignation from the Catholic Church and ministry, I stated to the bishop that I was leaving the priesthood because I could no longer offer the Mass, as it was contrary to the Word of God and to my conscience. This was in 1972. It was not long before I was baptized by immersion, began biblical studies and was ordained to the gospel ministry. For over twenty years I have walked in the freedom of which Jesus spoke in John 8: 'If the Son therefore shall make you free, ye shall be free indeed' (verse 36).

4

Simon Kottoor:
There Is Power in Christ's Atoning Blood

The love of Christ compels me to give testimony to my conversion from the Roman Catholic priesthood to the born-again life in Jesus Christ. For twenty-five years I was a Roman Catholic priest, strictly following the rituals of a system that enveloped me as a huge and indomitable fortress of darkness and ignorance of the written Word of God.

The Lord Teaches Me

I baptized many infants, pouring water on their heads. I officiated at public processions in honour and veneration of dead 'saints', holding their wooden images, even though the second commandment of God strictly forbids even the making of graven images. I offered the daily Mass, which I falsely believed was the repetition of the sacrifice of Jesus Christ on Calvary, and I believed that the bread and wine literally became Jesus' flesh and blood. Only later, when I had studied and prayed over the words of Jesus, as recorded in the Bible, were my eyes opened. The Lord taught me that there could not be a repetition of the consummated sacrifice on the cross, nor did Jesus literally change bread and wine into his body and blood when he instituted the last supper.

Very seriously, steadfastly, and sincerely, I sought the intercession of dead 'saints' and prayed for the dead in purgatory, not knowing the biblical teaching that there is only 'one God and one Mediator between God and men, the man Christ Jesus' (*1 Tim.* 2:5). He alone died in place of the believer and paid the full ransom for sin. This being true, we understand why there is no mention in the Bible of a place of expiation called purgatory, where souls are released through suffering and the prayers of those living on earth. As a sincere Catholic, I had great faith in the veneration of relics and the sacraments to which are attributed divine power when they are used for spiritual needs.

Only God Can Forgive Sin

While a priest, I heard many confessions and 'absolved' the sins of others, being ignorant of the biblical teaching that only God can forgive sin. The Bible says, 'And the scribes and the Pharisees began to reason, saying, Who is this which speaketh blasphemies? Who can forgive sins, but God alone?' (*Luke* 5:2). Remember this, 'If we confess our sins, he is faithful and just to forgive us our sins, and to cleanse us from all unrighteousness' (*1 John* 1:9).

I adhered to these and other beliefs and disciplines not only because I was born and brought up in that traditional system, but mainly because I was obliged to obey, for I believed the lie that 'outside the Roman Catholic Church there is no salvation'. The teaching of the Church called the *Magisterium*, based on tradition, was accepted as the final authority, not the written Word of God, the Bible (which was an unopened book, even for those studying for the priesthood).

No Peace Apart from God

My education for the Roman Catholic priesthood was in Rome. I took my Doctorate in Theology in 1954, and afterwards did post-graduate studies in economics in Canada. For eight years I was Professor of Economics at B.C.M. College for Women, Kottayam, India. I was also the principal of St Stephen's College, Uzhavoor, for nine years. These were high positions that gave me regard in society and material prosperity. During twenty-five years as a priest, I did not have spiritual joy or peace of soul even when performing the various rituals. There was an increasing sense of darkness and emptiness growing in my soul until I felt that there was no meaning in infant baptism, confession of sins, the 'real presence of Christ' in the Mass — or in any of the other rituals. I did not know what to do. I turned to smoking, drinking, gluttony, theatre attendance, and other secular activities in an effort to gain happiness and peace. But none of this could give me what my spirit needed. Those were years of agony and spiritual unrest. What I needed was eternal salvation.

Thy Word is a Light unto My Path

Somehow, I began to turn my attention to the Bible. Certain verses caught my attention. 'Heaven and earth shall pass away: but my words shall not pass away' (*Mark* 13:31). I realized that this was because 'All scripture is given by inspiration of God, and is profitable for doctrine, for reproof, for correction, for instruction in righteousness: That the man of God may be perfect, thoroughly furnished unto all good works' (2 *Tim.* 3:16–17).

I thank God for bringing into my life some born-again men who helped in my study. The Word of God became the 'lamp unto my feet' and the 'light unto my path'. I became convinced of the reason for my spiritual aridity and emptiness of soul: 'Whosoever transgresseth, and abideth not in the doctrine of Christ, hath not God. He that abideth in the doctrine of Christ, he hath both the Father and the Son' (2 *John* 1:9). Even though I had been very religious, I was not abiding in the doctrine of Christ. My eyes were opened to the doctrine of Christ as found in the Bible – the only 'power of God unto salvation'. The eternally meaningful question of Jesus in Matthew 16:26 seemed to ring in my ears: 'For what is a man profited, if he shall gain the whole world, and lose his own soul? or what shall a man give in exchange for his soul?'

Through the Word of God, I became convinced that it takes more than baptism to make a person a Christian. Infant baptism certainly cannot do it. An infant cannot believe, experience conviction, confess sin; cannot trust and accept Jesus Christ as personal Saviour. Soon, I realized my spiritual need and was convicted of my sin and of Christ's righteousness.

A New Creature

I praise the Lord for granting me the courage and strength to leave everything behind and trust Jesus Christ as my personal Saviour and Lord. The day was 5 April 1980. After I was born again by his Spirit and baptized in water, the Lord filled me with a divine peace, a joy of heart, and a meaning in my life. The emptiness of soul that had plagued me for so long vanished and I now know what it means to become a new creature. Old things are passed away; behold, all things are become new.

Satan, however, has not left me alone. He has been roaming about like a roaring lion. He began to make use of his agents to persecute me through physical assaults, isolation, ostracism, and false litigation against me. I have suffered the kinds of persecution described in Psalm 69:4, 8 and 12. Through all this, the Lord remained my comfort and strength. He has never failed nor forsaken me. His words in Psalm 27:10 and Luke 6:22–23 have given me added confidence, inspiration, and even joy.

The Lord blessed me with a Christian wife, formerly a nun for twelve years, and we have been living by faith and serving the Lord ever since. I have travelled to many places in India and abroad to preach the truth about the saving power of Jesus Christ and give the testimony of my conversion. I have visited many families and individuals in an effort to bring them to the Lord. It seems miraculous to realize how the Lord took my family and me from place to place in India in spite of the persecution. Finally, in 1987, He opened a way for me to take my family to America. Soon, through Dr Bart Brewer of Mission to Catholics International, we were introduced to Pastor Ted Duncan of Liberty Baptist Church in San Jose, California. I will ever remain grateful to these men for their benevolence and spiritual help to us. They were indeed good Samaritans.

My wife and I have been blessed with a son, Jimon, and a daughter, Jintomol. Our family resides in San Jose, and we worship at Liberty Baptist Church.

Dear Reader, look to Jesus Christ. There is power in his atoning blood to wash away your sins as he did mine. No one can limit the efficacy of the precious blood of Christ. Trust on him alone, and be 'justified freely by [God's] grace through the redemption that is in Christ Jesus' (*Rom*. 3:24).

5

Juan T. Sanz:
'Thou Knowest That I Love Thee'

I was born on 28 April 1930, in Somosiera, Madrid, Spain, the eighth child in a Roman Catholic family. I felt the call to the priesthood when I was thirteen, while listening to a sermon during the Mass (19 March 1943). For economic reasons, I did not enter the minor seminary of the diocese of Madrid until the academic year of 1945–6.

During the first five years of my course, I studied Latin and humanities. For the following three years, I studied philosophy, theology, and ethics. In September 1953, I began studying theology and ethics as basic subjects.

No seminarian could possess or read a Bible during his first eight years. On my twenty-first birthday a woman who would later be godmother at my first Mass gave me a Bible which, to her surprise, she had to take home until I was twenty-four years old and started my theological studies. So my interest in knowing more about the Bible would be more of a curiosity than a necessity.

My First Mass

I was ordained a priest on 14 July 1957, and on the 18th of the same month I celebrated my first Mass in my home town. My first parish church was La Neriuela, Madrid. I took possession on 23 August 1957, and continued there until 1959 when, due to my parents' health, I resigned and was assigned coadjutor to the parish church in the neighborhood of Canillejas, Madrid.

I took my parents and my sister with me to this new post, where both the parish priest and the parishioners received us with open arms. But half a year had not gone by when my fellowship with the parish priest gradually began to deteriorate due to his fundamentalist and conservative attitude concerning the content of the preaching, the administration of the sacraments, the liturgy of the Mass, and devotion to the Virgin Mary and the saints.

Why did I have to preach what the parish priest wanted? Why did I have to hear the confession of the penitents before celebrating Mass, as if this were the expiation of their sins? Why was specific devotion to Mary and the saints allowed during the celebration of the Mass? Why use Latin in the Mass, and administration of the sacraments, if the parishioners could not understand it?

In my first parish I had used Spanish in various parts of the Mass, and at funerals and baptisms. This so pleased the vast majority of parishioners that their attendance and participation in worship gradually increased.

Reform in the Parish

After two years, I spoke to my parish priest about my use of Spanish and the Bible in my previous pastoral work. Later he informed me that, with the Bishop's permission, we would be using Spanish during much of the liturgy and sacraments but that the Sunday and quarterly preaching would have to remain unchanged, even though I thought that they moralized too much and consequently were not very biblical. The themes of the preaching were chosen by a group of conservative priests with the aim that all clerical diocesans would preach on the same theme at a particular Sunday Mass. Even so I managed to 'restyle' the proposed themes, giving them a new slant towards Christ. When my parish priest heard about this, he told me, to my great surprise that he would substitute for me in the pulpit when he could, leaving me to officiate at the Mass

In those difficult days of my priestly ministry, I used the Bible as my bedside book and searched more and more for its truthful, profound, and eternal message of salvation, for me and for the rest of the world.

The Lord Answers

One day, the Lord answered all my questions when he led me to read and understand chapter 3 of the Gospel of John. God's love and promises now became to me and would henceforth be the only rule, power, authority, and mirror to my soul. But, had they not always been so for me? In one way they had, but now they were in another way, since God had regenerated me by his Word and Spirit: 'For God so loved the world, that he gave his only-begotten Son, that whosoever believeth in him should not perish, but have everlasting life' (*John* 3:16). Therefore God was my Father and his Son, Jesus Christ, was my own perfect Saviour. This was something completely new for me. A big change had taken place in my heart; I felt as if I had been an actor before men, like a blind man guiding other blind men.

In the summer of 1964, I asked the Lord to tell me what to do with my life, as I could no longer continue in the Roman Catholic Church. Its hierarchy forced me to preach 'another gospel', different from the message of salvation by grace through faith, found only in Christ.

But when and how could I leave my priestly ministry? Who would support my parents and my sister financially? If I gave up my post for the sake of faith and conscience, would I find understanding and support from the Bishop? How would the Protestants, to whom I was thinking of going for advice, receive me?

In the spring of 1965, I heard about the 'desertion' of a priest, also from Madrid, and a superior of the seminary, who, with the help of the pastor of an Evangelical Church, had left the Roman Catholic Church and had gone abroad to study Protestantism in a European, Protestant University. So my colleague's attitude and determination gave me the answer as to how I could leave the priesthood and know in a deeper way the gospel of the liberty of God's children.

With this aim, I contacted the German Church, La Iglesia de los Alemanes, in Madrid. They gave me Pastor Luis Ruiz Poveda's telephone number. As soon as I told him that I was a priest with problems of conscience and faith, he advised me to stop the conversation and arranged that we should meet at a certain place and time, as his telephone was frequently tapped by the police. And that is what we did.

Mortal Sin or New Life?

Until my way became clear, I felt as if my spiritual and psychological life were collapsing. In terms of Roman Catholic doctrine, I was living constantly in a state of 'mortal sin', because I formally doubted my faith, I did not search for the pardon of this and other sins in the sacrament of penitence, I searched for biblical truth in Protestantism and not in my Bishop and theology professors, I rejected the Roman Catholic ecclesiastical hierarchy and authority, I rejected the doctrinal authority of my church concerning the Bible, it seemed to me that the aural confession of sins robbed God of the right and power which he alone has in his person and through the actions of his Son, Jesus Christ, and finally the celebration of the Mass seemed to me a supplanting of the merits of Christ on the cross.

Did this mean my pastoral ministry was at an end? The Lord told me by his Word that it did not. But I found myself fighting against the Lord's will, against my Roman Catholic mentality, and against my stubborn pride. This inner battle affected my health and sleep, and produced many fears. In the end it required me to renounce everything for love of Christ, and for my own eternal salvation.

I Respond to the Lord's Grace

At the end of the tunnel of anguish and fear, the Lord Jesus invited me to respond to him as the Apostle Peter had done for the third time near the lake. It was these words that I had already chosen as my motto for life before being ordained as a priest: 'Lord, thou knowest all things; thou knowest that I love thee' (*John* 21:17).

Thus the Lord led me out of the shadows of Roman Catholicism into the light of the gospel of grace. 'For by grace are ye saved through faith; and that not of yourselves: it is the gift of God: not of works, lest any man should boast' (*Eph.* 2:8–9).

6

Vincent O'Shaughnessy: From Dead Religion to New Life in Christ

I was born and raised on a farm in West Limerick, Ireland, and the memories of my childhood are happy ones. The youngest of seven children (three sisters and three brothers), I had lots of relatives to visit or to receive as visitors on Sundays after Mass. No one ever missed Mass on Sunday in those days in Ireland, unless they were seriously ill. Such a lapse was designated a mortal sin, meaning a deadly sin, deserving of hell, should one die with it unconfessed and unforgiven by a priest. The priests were revered, even idolized. I decided I would like to be a priest myself.

As a very small boy, I remember rolling out of bed each morning to my knees to say my morning prayers, beginning with the *Morning Offering*, which my mother taught me, together with the *Our Father* and *Hail Mary*. I still remember the *Morning Offering* going like this:

'O Jesus, through the most pure heart of Mary', which meant to me that to get to Jesus, I had to go through Mary. I also have a vivid picture of kneeling in the kitchen each evening to pray the Rosary with the family, but most of all I remember that the trimmings to the Rosary were longer than the Rosary itself. Everyone that had any problem in the neighbourhood had to be prayed for with three *Hail Marys* each time, and all the deceased relatives likewise.

I Become a Priest

So I applied to St Patrick's College, a missionary college and seminary in Thurles, County Tipperary. I was accepted and began my six years of studies for the priesthood, which consisted of two years of philosophy and four years dogmatic theology and moral theology, plus Canon Law and other subjects. We did no real study of God's Word, just an academic smattering about the Bible, but nothing of any depth or consequence. I often regret that no one ever told me to study God's Word during those six long years. However, without being born again, it probably would not have interested me. I would have lacked understanding, as the eyes of my understanding had not been opened up to the Word of God.

The long-awaited day of ordination finally came on 15 June 1953. It was a memorable occasion with a big reception for family and friends. The celebration continued through the next day, the day of the first Mass, when most of the parish people showed up for the young priest's first blessing.

Going to America

Following three months vacation in my homeland, I set sail for New York with several other recently-ordained priests, destined for various places in the United States. My first assignment was to the Cathedral in downtown Sacramento, California, one block from the state capitol. I began my priestly duties with much zeal and commitment to the work of the ministry; I was determined to do the very best job that I could do and to be the very best priest I could be. I was assigned a room on the third floor of the Cathedral rectory, which had just been vacated by a man who had a common problem among Catholic priests, namely alcoholism. It took me several trips to the garbage container in the backyard to get rid of all the empty bottles I found in drawers and closets. I was grieved because at this time I was a 'teetotaller' and belonged to an Irish organization called 'The Pioneer Total Abstinence Association'. (We identified ourselves by wearing a little red heart-shaped pin. When Irish people saw someone wearing such an emblem, they would not offer him alcoholic drinks.)

Humbled in the Confessional

At the Cathedral, I remember spending long hours in the confessional, not wanting to walk out of the confessional while people were still waiting in line. However, when the allocated time was up, walking out of the 'box' did not seem to bother the other priests. The result was that I used to show up late for scheduled meals and was made fun of by the others for my service to the latecomers, especially the Mexican-Americans. God gave me special love for these humble, unassuming people, who in turn loved their padre as they knelt and kissed my hand. This experience touched me and humbled me.

From the Cathedral, I went to fill a vacancy at another parish in the suburbs that had an Irish staff. My new parish priest (in the States we call them 'pastor') was a semi-invalid with three assistants, but I soon found out that the real acting pastor was the Monsignor's sister, who was the housekeeper. She answered all the door calls and phone calls and routed them to her brother, whether they asked for him or not. The kitchen was out of bounds and so was the dining room, unless one was invited by the housekeeper to come in for the meals. One day, she chased one of the assistant priests out of 'her kitchen' with a carving knife, causing him to grab a chair to keep from being stabbed.

I remained in that environment for five years while the old pastor grew progressively worse in health. This caused me to have more and more responsibility in running the parish and, believe it or not, the housekeeper took a liking to me, and we got along well for the rest of my time there.

Heresy of Activism

I soon got caught up in what I call the heresy of activism, which caused my spiritual life to suffer the consequences. I still spent time in prayer before and after Mass and read the breviary (the official prayers for the clergy) daily. I prepared my sermons on Saturday from the outline supplied by the diocese. I enjoyed preaching, as I had been trained how to appeal to the emotions of the soul. I had no training and no idea how to minister in the Spirit or to the spirit of the people. I made the people feel good, and on that score I was considered successful.

'Are You Saved?'

About five years into my priesthood, God spoke to me through a little child, but I did not pay any attention to what this child was saying to me. I was standing in front of the church. I think that I may have been waiting for a funeral to arrive. I had the vestments on for the funeral Mass. There was nobody around except a little black boy who looked like he was 3–4 years old. He walked up to me and around me, all the while sizing me up with his big eyes. Finally he spoke, saying, 'Who are you? You a preacher?' Then he walked around me again, looked me right in the eye, and said, 'Are you saved?' I do not remember what my response or my reaction was to him, perhaps one of pity or prejudice. That little boy had asked me the all-important question of life and I had no idea what he was talking about. Obviously, he understood what it meant to be saved and God was using him to get my attention, but to no avail. If I only knew then what I found out twelve years later, I would have had to admit honestly to that little boy that I was not saved. I was 45 years old before I knew what the little boy was saying to me, before I knew what it meant to be saved, to be a born-again Christian.

The Role of a Priest

I had applied for a transfer and found myself out in a farming community. It was not long after that I welcomed Sister Yvonne and Sister N. to our parish in August 1968. From the moment we met, there was instant rapport between Sister Yvonne and me, as though we had been long-time friends. Our relationship was kept on a professional level. We both enjoyed conversation and sharing views on various subjects. One day, in the midst of a discussion about a book, I asked Sister Yvonne, 'Sister, how do you see me functioning in the ministry of the priesthood? And I want you to be brutally honest with me.' Her response to my question blew me away. She said, 'Father, I see you doing all the right things, I hear you saying all the right words from the pulpit, I see you fulfilling the role of a priest.' In other words, she viewed me in the character of a priest. Although she did not realize the full effect of her words, it was the turning point in my life. To me it spoke of role-playing on the stage of life. Shakespeare says, 'All the world's a stage.' I no longer wanted to be a priest performing on the stage of life; now I wanted off the stage as quickly as possible. Thus, began long months of agonizing.

Sister Yvonne Resigns

The final class for the sisters before Christmas vacation came, and I had been asking Sister Yvonne for the programme schedule for the coming new year. It was the last class for 1968 and she still had not given me the schedule that I requested. She fumbled with her handbag, pulled out an envelope, and handed it to me saying, 'I shouldn't really do this, but I believe you deserve to know.' The letter in the envelope was dated May 1968 and was addressed to her Superior of the Order, the Sisters of the Holy Family. In her letter she was submitting her resignation from the sisterhood. However, inasmuch as she had made vows for a year, she offered to finish out the year if her leaving would cause a lot of inconvenience. This is how she got reassigned to Mount Shasta, California, rather than the large convent in the San Francisco Bay area where she had been first assigned. As I read this letter, which meant that she would not be coming back to my parish, the tears started rolling down my cheeks. She said, 'What's the matter with you?' I said something like, 'I don't know, I guess I'm just in shock.' The children began to arrive for class and I got out of there, leaving Yvonne to face her class. That was the last I saw of Yvonne for several weeks. She departed for the convent at Mount Shasta the next day. That Christmas was a lonely, dismal one, with lots of snow causing many problems. The truth of the saying, 'Absence makes the heart grow fonder', became very evident, as I finally had to admit to God and to myself that I was in love with Yvonne. Obviously she did not want anything to do with that kind of a relationship because of my being a priest and her high regard for my calling. She did not want to be responsible before God for my leaving the priesthood.

I Leave the Priesthood

I went through a lot of agonizing, crying out to God for direction in my life. Should I leave the priesthood? Could I change my priesthood for the better? I called the best missioner that I knew to come and hold a mission in an effort to bring a spiritual revival to my life and to the parish. The mission was held the first week of Lent, but the message rang hollow; it was empty, devoid of a heart for God, as Paul says: 'Having a form of godliness, but denying the power thereof; from such turn away' (2 *Tim*. 3:5). My mind was made up. I was through. I wrote to Yvonne to tell her about my decision and asked if I could come to talk with her. We had dinner together. I convinced her that I was leaving regardless of our relationship ever developing. She said, 'I was wrong to try to talk you out of your decision. But if you leave, you need to do so apart from me. You have to know it is God's will.' I wrote to my Bishop, told him of my decision, and requested that he apply for a dispensation to Rome so that we could be married in the Catholic Church.

Yvonne and I Marry

I arrived in Oakland, where Yvonne had an apartment on Lake Merritt. I moved in and she moved back to her mother's house in Pleasant Hill. This was a peaceful place for me where I began a healing process from the awful trauma that followed my final decision. I spent my days praying for a job and filling out applications. One day a friend at the Probation Department, a former Dominican priest, gave me an application that came across his desk from Colusa County. I filled it out, mailed it, went for an interview, and got the job. Yvonne and I were married and moved to the town of Colusa. The dispensation finally came and the Catholic Church blessed our marriage. Yvonne got a job as Director of the Confraternity of Christian Doctrine for the parish. Please remember that we were committed Catholics and that is how we were determined to remain. However, each time we came home from being at Mass, we felt so dry, so thirsty, and hungry for the reality of God, for some spiritual food to chew on and digest, but it seemed nowhere to be found. God had given us jobs, a beautiful home, and now a precious daughter, Kelly Ann. We were so happy and filled with gratitude to God for all his goodness to us. We were seeking for a deeper and more meaningful relationship with him.

We Are Born Again

One day we obtained a book about a priest who was born again by the Holy Spirit. This was all very new to me. The book was a testimony of his life and his meeting with God. Not long after reading this little book, Yvonne and I were invited to a meeting where a nun shared her testimony of God's power to save, and how she experienced the new birth. I felt the Lord had touched my heart and was speaking to me. When the invitation was given to come and receive the Lord as Saviour, Yvonne and I were the first to go forward. We prayed that Christ would be Lord of every area of our lives, and immediately we began to feel the difference. It was at this point, I believe, that I was born again; I had assurance of salvation and peace that my sins were forgiven. Our prayer life had a new meaning and reality. The Bible, the Word of God, began to come alive and be more meaningful as we began to read and study it.

Saved by Grace, Not by Works

We started attending a Bible study and dipping into the Word of God deeper and deeper. As we did so, we found that many of the things we had been taught as Catholics did not line up with God's Word. In the final analysis, the Roman Catholic Church teaches a gospel of works (that is, salvation through man's own efforts to lead a good life and to do penance for sins, as if Jesus Christ had not paid for it all with his blood shed on Calvary's cross). The Scripture makes it very clear that salvation is a free gift of God, received by faith; 'For by grace are ye saved through faith; and that not of yourselves; it is the gift of God, not of works, lest any man should boast' (*Eph.* 2:8–9).

Jesus Alone Is Saviour

We have come to see the need for Catholics to separate themselves from the errors of Catholicism, even as we have. The Lord Jesus has really blessed our lives as we have sought to serve him. We have never been so happy. The Lord has blessed us with two beautiful daughters and has opened many doors to minister God's Word and to pray for people.

Our prayer for all who read this testimony is that they may know Christ and the power of his resurrection. Why not seek the Lord Jesus Christ with all your heart, accepting that he and he alone is the Saviour?

7

José A. Fernandez:
I Was Blind, Now I See

I was born blind, not physically but spiritually, in 1899, in one of the most mountainous and inaccessible regions of Asturias, rightly called the 'Spanish Switzerland'. My parents were devout Roman Catholics who believed implicitly everything that the Roman Catholic Church believed and taught.

They had, indeed, a blind faith, which they transmitted to their seventeen children. Roman Catholicism permeated the hearts, the minds, and even the bodies of the children as they grew up. It was a home where babies were nursed and nourished with love and devotion to Mary and the saints; where later on the children were impressed with the value of medals, scapulars, beads, and holy pictures; and where the priest's word was law and had to be obeyed.

As early as I can remember, I had a strong inclination toward everything connected with the Church and the priest, whom I had been taught to regard as a superhuman being devoid of the ordinary human needs and weaknesses. My greatest delight was to serve as an altar boy, considering it a great privilege and honour to rise early in the morning and walk two miles in the snow through mountainous terrain in order to assist the priest at the Mass. At the age of seven, I was able to recite the prayers of the Mass in Latin.

Blind Faith in the Church

Family devotions, consisting of the recitation of the Rosary and a long litany of prayers to all the patron Saints, were held every night without exception. The whole family, including the small children, gathered in the kitchen, which also served as living room. We formed quite a congregation! When my father took the beads from his pocket, it was the signal for all of us to go down on our knees on the bare stone floor, ready for the coming ordeal, which usually lasted forty minutes.

The recitation of the beads, consisting of the Apostles' Creed, fifty-three 'Hail Marys', six repetitions of 'Glory Be', five of 'Our Father', one 'Hail, Holy Queen', and the Litany of the Blessed Virgin, was trying enough. Far more so was what followed, a seemingly endless series of prayers to the different 'Virgins', Angels, and Saints noted for their special advocacy and protection in all circumstances and vicissitudes of life.

The Worship of Images

My early religious life was centered on one main event during the year: the Festival of the Virgin of Dawn, commemorating the festival of the Assumption of Mary into heaven on 15 August.

The Virgin of Dawn was the patroness of the region. According to a legend, the virgin appeared to a certain shepherd on a nearby mountain called 'Alba' or 'Dawn'. A sanctuary was erected on the spot to honour the apparition. Every year a religious pageant was enacted, and the shrine was visited by thousands of pilgrims from far and near. The statue of the Virgin, attired in splendid regalia, was carried in procession through the mountainside, to the acclaim and veneration of the devotees who came either to pray for a miracle or to thank her for the miracles already performed. Each region in Spain claims at least one such miraculous Virgin. Fatima is reproduced hundreds of times!

Although Roman Catholic theology distinguishes between the statue and the person it represents, in practice that distinction is theoretical only. In spite of the teaching of the Catechism, there is no doubt in my mind that both I and those simple mountain people really worshipped the image. In our belief, a supernatural power was attached to the physical part of the figure, for it was not even a statue in the proper sense of the word. It consisted of a few sticks arranged so as to provide the skeleton on which a face was placed. The figure

47

was then dressed in silk and gold. I was shocked beyond words when one day I saw the altar ladies undress the statue and noticed that the virgin of my dreams was only a dummy. That mental picture has remained with me ever since.

Having observed my religious inclinations, the parish priest approached me with the idea of studying for the priesthood. Guided by the exalted opinion I had of that profession, I yielded readily to his persuasion, much to the joy and satisfaction of my deeply religious father and the consternation of my equally religious mother, who opposed the idea on the grounds of her maternal instinct and love.

Friar and Priest

At the age of twelve I left my home, father, mother, brothers, and sisters, never to see them again. The glory of the priestly life, the enchantments of the monastery, and the salvation of my soul envisaged on the horizon of my mind overcame the natural sadness that came over me as I took leave of my family and the scenes of my childhood.

I was sent to a high school located in the province of Valladolid. The high school was conducted by priests of the Dominican Order for the purpose of training young boys already set aside by their parents for the priesthood.

During the four years of my stay there, I not only studied the high school subjects but became proficient in the large Roman Catholic Catechism. Romanism took hold of me body and soul; the seed of intolerance was then sown in my soul, as the Catechism insisted that there was only one true Church of Jesus Christ, outside of which there was no salvation. That Church was the 'Holy Roman Catholic and Apostolic Church'. There God was presented to my young mind as a stern judge ready to render to us according to our sins, an angry God that had to be appeased by good works, penances and mortifications.

During the first two years of my training, my life was exemplary in the observance of every rule and in the diligent attention and care to my studies. I was honoured on several occasions with special awards. From this 'Apostolic' School, I was sent to the Dominican Novitiate in Avila, and in the famous monastery of Santo Tomas I was invested with the black and white habit of the Dominican Order at the age of sixteen.

A Time of Torture

One full year was devoted to intensive study of the Rule and Constitution of the Order, rigid observance of the Rule, and chanting the Office of the Virgin, under the constant vigilance of the Novice Master. It was a year of trial and probation, which only the strongest characters could survive. Fasting was prescribed from 14 September to Easter. The Master carefully censored the incoming and outgoing mail. All contact with the outside world was prohibited. No conversation or communication could be held between the priest and the professed members of the monastery. Auricular confession was obligatory every week, and this was generally held on Saturday and had to be made to the same Novice Master who was at the same time our superior and constant supervisor. It is not difficult to imagine the anxiety and mental torture that such unmerciful practice, since changed by the Canon Law of the Church, inflicted on the young novices, who literally dreaded the approach of Saturday. But the dream and anticipation of one day becoming a full-fledged friar provided me with the courage needed to complete that year of probation and absolute self-renunciation.

The day of partial liberation came on 8 September 1917, the Feast of the Nativity of the Virgin Mary, when I made my profession as a member of the Dominican Order. The next four years were spent in Santo Tomas College, adjoining the novitiate. From the time I left home at twelve until I finished college at twenty-one, I had not spoken to a woman. Womanhood was presented to our young minds as something evil, and on numerous occasions the religious instructors related to us stories of saints who never looked at their mothers' faces, citing this as an example of chastity to be imitated by us.

Studies in America and Ordination

After four years of college, I was sent to the United States to study theology and learn English. I spent three years in the Dominican Theological Seminary in Louisiana and some time at Notre Dame University. Soon after my ordination to the priesthood in 1924, I was sent as assistant pastor to one of the largest Roman Catholic churches in New Orleans, Louisiana. I served in that capacity for nine years; in 1932, I was appointed pastor of the same church at the age of thirty-two.

For six years I laboured untiringly, zealously and with great success. The church grew in membership, attendance at religious services, reception of the sacraments, and even in material goods. When I became pastor, the parochial school had an enrolment of about 450 pupils; two years later, there were more than a thousand pupils. I made it possible for hundreds of poor children to receive free religious education.

The Dominican Order honoured me with the office of Superior of the Dominican House connected with the church. My community was composed of five priests and two lay brothers. I was also the Father Confessor of several convents of nuns, facts that prove the high esteem in which the Archbishop, the congregation, and my religious superiors held me. I was indeed a 'Pharisee of the Pharisees', in great need of a personal encounter with the living Christ.

A Penitent Soul

During the last years of my pastorate, I began to doubt the validity of some of the doctrines of the Roman Catholic Church. The first thing that I doubted, and rejected, was the power of the priest to forgive sins in confession. Neither could I make myself believe in the doctrine of the transubstantiation, or the real physical bodily presence of Christ in the host (wafer) and the chalice (cup). My faith in the Roman Catholic Church weakened. I felt that I could no longer remain a hypocrite. I was entertaining the idea of leaving the priesthood. God intervened and provided the occasion, by means of human agents. The Master General of the Dominican Order issued orders from Rome to the effect that Spanish Dominican priests in Louisiana should leave their churches and turn them over to the American Dominicans. Some were ordered to Spain, others to the Philippines. I resigned myself to abandon the parish without any protest, feeling that the hand of God was in this new turn of events. However, I refused to leave the country of my adoption, which I had learned to love. I left the priesthood and took the road that leads to the gutter of sin, but somewhere along that road God took pity on me and saved me from a disastrous end. For a year and a half a terrific struggle went on within my soul. I felt tempted to turn away from God and everything sacred. But then I would remember the words that came from the depths of Peter's heart, 'Lord, to whom shall we go? Thou hast the words of eternal life.'

The world, with all its pleasures and allurements, could not fill the vacuum in my soul. After vainly trying to find happiness in the things of the world, and wishing to save my soul, I took the road that led to a monastery in Florida. It was my purpose to consecrate my life to God in the solitude of the monastic life, to bury myself within the four walls of that sacred precinct, to work for and earn my own salvation. In the seclusion of a monastery, I thought God would surely give me that assurance of salvation and the happiness of soul that I was seeking. That was my purpose, but God had other designs for me. From now on, God's hand leading me was manifest. It was in the monastery that I became acquainted with Evangelical Christianity.

For a while, I worked in the library of the monastery. There was in that library a particular cabinet with the inscription, 'Forbidden Books'. Curiosity got the better of me. One day I took the key, opened the cabinet, and saw six or seven books. I read them all, one by one. They were religious books dealing with the evidences against Roman Catholicism as the true Church of Jesus Christ.

I also began to read the Bible. Until then, the Bible did not mean much to me personally. It was indeed the inspired Word of God, but I was told that the ordinary human mind is not able to understand its true meaning. I believed that an infallible authority was necessary to impart the meaning of what was in the mind of the Holy Spirit when he inspired the sacred writers. I preferred to read the Word of God as understood by this infallible authority and as found in the Roman Catholic missals and prayer books.

Gradually, the reading of the Bible became a source of comfort and inspiration in the solitude of the monastery, and I began to understand the real meaning of certain passages of the Bible to which I had not paid particular attention in the past.

I was particularly impressed with the following verses as I read them in the Bible: 'For there is one God, and one mediator between God and men, the man Christ Jesus; who gave himself a ransom for all, to be testified in due time' (*1 Tim.* 2:5–6); 'Grace be with all them that love our Lord Jesus Christ in sincerity. Amen' (*Eph.* 6:24); 'And they said, Believe on the Lord Jesus Christ, and thou shalt be saved, and thy house' (*Acts* 16:31); 'Now the Spirit speaketh expressly, that in the latter times some shall depart from the faith, giving heed to seducing spirits, and doctrines of devils; speaking lies in hypocrisy; having their conscience seared with a hot iron; forbidding to marry, and commanding to abstain from meats, which God hath created to be received with thanksgiving of them which believe and know the truth. For every creature of God is good, and nothing to be refused, if it be received with thanksgiving' (*1 Tim.* 4:1–3).

The seed of the Word of God was then planted in the garden of my soul. It is true that I tried to smother it, but that little seed was to grow and bear fruit in due time. Teaching church history to the young monks, I became acquainted with the corruption of the Roman Catholic Church, both in doctrine and in practice; and in my heart I felt a deep admiration for the courageous leaders of the Reformation. After two years in the monastery, I had not found the peace of mind or the happiness of soul that I was seeking. What should I do next?

An American Soldier

Not wishing to go on living in those surroundings, anxious to be useful in some way to humanity, and knowing that my adopted country was at war, I did the most honourable thing I could: I enlisted in the U.S. Army. Divine Providence again guided me. After my basic training, I was sent to the Military Intelligence Training Center at Camp Ritchie, Maryland. The men selected to attend this Intelligence School were highly educated. We had to take orders from corporals and sergeants who for the most part in their civilian life did nothing, perhaps, but sweep streets or wash dishes. But they could use strong language, and the stronger the language, the more stripes. But I thank God for these men, for they fitted me for my future Christian ministry as they taught me humility, obedience, discipline, and spiritual democracy.

I was assigned for awhile to the Chaplain's office. The Chaplain, Major Herman J. Kregel, was a minister of the Dutch Reformed Church with a brilliant mind and a heart of gold. I loved to listen to his sermons on Sunday mornings, for he was a fluent and interesting speaker. Under his guidance, while my mind was reacting favourably to his full and lucid explanations in doctrinal matters, my heart became captivated by the example of his conduct, his charity, unselfishness, broad-mindedness and naturalness. For the first time I realized that a Protestant minister could be happy and sincere in his faith and work. In the American Army proselytizing of members of another faith by a chaplain is not done. The relations between the Protestant chaplain and myself were cordial in the usual chaplain-soldier relationship, but no more. He had no objections to my attending Protestant services. After all, the right to worship when and where one pleased was one of the things we were fighting for.

Salvation by Faith Alone

One Sunday Major Kregel preached on Paul's doctrine of salvation by faith alone. Up to that time, I had discarded practically every doctrine and practice characteristic of the Roman Catholic Church, but I had clung tenaciously to the belief in salvation by works. After the service, I went to his office to let him know how I felt about his 'heretical' statements. Armed with the text from James 2:24, 'Ye see then how that by works a man is justified, and not by faith only.' I arrogantly and ignorantly said to him: 'If what you said is right, then James is wrong; if James is right, you and Paul are wrong. Otherwise, you must admit there is a contradiction in the Bible.' He replied, 'José, there can be no contradictions in the Bible, for the Holy Spirit is its only author, and the Spirit cannot contradict Himself.' With that, of course, I fully agreed.

'Now,' he continued, 'when Paul says that salvation is by faith alone, he speaks from the point of view of God, who reads our minds and sees our hearts. So far as God is concerned, we are saved the moment that we believe. But this belief, please notice, is a faith of trust and not just a mental assent to a few doctrinal statements.' Never before had I heard faith defined that way. 'On the other hand,' he went on, 'when James states that salvation is by works also, he speaks from the point of view of men who, being unable to read our minds or see our hearts, must have something visible and tangible by which to judge whether or not we are saved. As far as men are concerned, we are saved when we produce good works. But good works are not the root; they are the result of salvation.'

The explanation was unique; I had never heard it before. I fully agreed with it. The last mental barrier had been removed. I became an 'intellectual' believer and promised the Lord to give my life to the Protestant ministry when my time in the Army was at an end. But I was not yet fit for that ministry. My mind had been converted, but my heart remained untouched. A true conversion must effect a change not only of mind but, above all, of the heart. I believed in every fundamental truth of the Bible, but I had not surrendered my heart to Christ.

A Sinner Saved by Grace

I prayed for light, studied for information, and on my days off visited the different churches in Maryland and Pennsylvania to find out which one appealed to me most on biblical grounds. During one of my journeys through the churches of Baltimore, I met one who was going to be my life partner, a deeply religious lady of the Baptist communion. She possessed a winning personality, a delightful sense of humour, and a fine Christian heart. Our short courtship ended in a most happy union brought about by a Baptist minister in a Baptist church. The good lady could not give me salvation, but the merciful Lord was going to grant it to me six months after our marriage. The Bible teaches believers not to marry unbelievers. I did not know this Bible command at the time I married.

In the fall of 1944, I was assigned as interpreter for South American officers studying the military science of mechanized cavalry at Fort Riley, Kansas. While doing army reconnaissance, I also engaged in spiritual reconnaissance, searching for the truth.

One Saturday night, I attended a Salvation Army open-air service on a street corner of Junction City, Kansas. At first my attitude toward the meeting was one of indifference and even scorn. But as the meeting went on, I was being supernaturally drawn to give earnest attention. My effort was rewarded. A young Salvation Army lady gave a stirring message that ended by appealing to those standing by to believe on the all-sufficient sacrifice of Christ, to respond to his grace. Then she quoted the words of Jesus as recorded in John 5:24: 'Verily, verily, I say unto you, He that heareth my word, and believeth on him that sent me, hath everlasting life, and shall not come into condemnation; but is passed from death unto life.'

At that moment, I felt myself passing from death to life and under the influence of a supernatural force. I went down on my knees, confessed Christ as the Lord of my life, and received him as my Saviour. What happened, how it happened, I cannot tell; all I can do is repeat with the blind man of the Gospel, 'Whereas I was blind, now I see' (*John* 9:25). In the face of the transformed life, there can be no denial of the power of the Holy Spirit. Something happened in my life; I am not the same man. I love the things that I used to hate and hate the things that I used to love. For the unregenerate man and woman, this may seem foolishness because 'the natural man receiveth not the things of the Spirit of God: for they are foolishness unto him: neither can he know them, because they are spiritually discerned' (*1 Cor.* 2:14). My life since then has been a public testimony to the transforming power of the Holy Spirit. I have been saved by God's grace.

Gospel Minister

Soon after our marriage, my wife and I went to live in Blue Ridge Summit on the mountain range dividing Maryland from Pennsylvania. The pastor of the Presbyterian Church was the Rev. C. P. Muyskens, a college classmate of Chaplain Kregel and, like him, a former minister of the Dutch Reformed denomination. Worshipping regularly in his church, we became acquainted with his sterling qualities as preacher and pastor. Visiting him at his home, we were impressed with his Christian family life. He did not leave his religion in the pulpit but took it home with him. In him I found the inspiration, guidance, and encouragement that I needed during the transition period from soldier to gospel minister.

On 24 April 1945, while still in the Army, I was ordained a Presbyterian minister at the Hawley Memorial Presbyterian Church of Blue Ridge Summit. Two months later, I was given the piece of paper I was avidly waiting for, an honourable discharge from the Army! That fall, I entered Princeton Theological Seminary, where I studied for, and obtained, the degree of Master of Theology. My year there was without doubt the happiest of my life. There I found spiritual uplift, Christian fellowship, intellectual growth, and deep religious experience. It was indeed, as in the case of the Apostle Paul, an 'Arabia' for me. When I compared conditions there with those of my Catholic seminary days, the difference was striking. Fear, regimentation, and constant supervision had given way to love, joy, and the freedom of the children of God.

8

John Zanon:
I Found Christ the Only Mediator

I was born in 1910 to poor but devout Roman Catholic parents living in northern Italy. Following my ordination by Cardinal Rossi, 29 June 1935, I was sent to the United States.

A few years after this, I received a table radio as a birthday gift. To my surprise and joy, I was able to receive a few Protestant programmes, and I loved their messages and songs from the very beginning. The thing that impressed me the most was that they put a great emphasis on the Bible. It seemed to me these preachers were really fulfilling Christ's mandate: 'to preach the gospel . . . for it is the power of God unto salvation to everyone who believeth' (*Rom.* 1:15–16). In an attempt to prove how right I was in being in the Roman Catholic Church and how wrong those were who were outside of it, I began to read the Bible earnestly and prayerfully. The more I read and the harder I prayed to God, the more clearly I understood how wrong the Church of Rome was. In the Gospel of John I read, 'But as many as received him, to them gave he power to become the sons of God' (*John* 1:12); 'For God so loved the world, that he gave his only begotten Son, that whosoever believeth in him should not perish, but have everlasting life' (*John* 3:16). The Bible could not be clearer in this all-important matter of our salvation.

Being a Roman Catholic priest did not assure the salvation of my soul. I came to realize that my zeal and good works as a priest could not save me, because I read in the Bible: 'For by grace are ye saved through faith; and that not of yourselves: it is the gift of God: not of works, lest any man should boast' (*Eph.* 2:8–9).

Teachings not in the Bible

This shook my faith in Roman Catholic teachings. Up until now I had blindly accepted all of Rome's teachings. A Catholic has no choice: either he accepts Rome's doctrines without question, or he is excommunicated. Because I was beginning to doubt everything, I started searching the Scriptures more diligently than ever. I discovered that the sacrifice of Jesus Christ on the cross was all-sufficient, 'By the which will we are sanctified through the offering of the body of Jesus Christ once for all' (*Heb.* 10:10); 'For by one offering he hath perfected for ever them that are sanctified' (*Heb.* 10:14); 'Who needeth not daily, as those high priests, to offer up sacrifice, first for his own sins, and then for the people's: for this he did once, when he offered up himself' (*Heb.* 7:27). Then there is no need of Mass, confession, or Purgatory.

Go to Jesus, Not to Rome

I began to realize that all these doctrines of the so-called 'only true Church' were nothing but Roman inventions. Pursuing my studies further, I learned that devotions to Mary, the mother of our Saviour, and to the saints, were not even mentioned in the Bible. Mary herself directed the attendants at the marriage feast of Cana to go to Jesus: 'His mother saith unto the servants, whatsoever he saith unto you, do it' (*John* 2:5). Christ invites us to come directly to him and not through the saints as the Roman Church teaches: 'Come unto me, all ye that labour and are heavy laden, and I will give you rest' (*Matt.* 11:28); 'Jesus saith unto him, I am the way, the truth, and the life: no man cometh unto the Father, but by me' (*John* 14:6); 'If ye shall ask any thing in my name, I will do it' (*John* 14:14). And Paul, divinely inspired, wrote: 'For there is one God, and one mediator between God and men, the man Christ Jesus' (*1 Tim.* 2:5).

Once again I had to conclude from my Bible study that all the thousand and one devotions to the saints were inventions of Rome. For the first time in my life it became crystal clear that the teachings of the Roman Catholic Church were wrong. I thanked the Lord for enlightening my mind. I had no choice but to leave the Roman Catholic Church. I began formulating my plans, but the decision frightened me. I knew my parents and brothers would be hurt and the Catholics would feel I had disgraced them. It would also cost me many life-long friends, security, prestige, and a comfortable life. I delayed and prayed. The voice of the Lord came clear and firm, 'He that loveth father or mother more than me is not worthy of me: and he that loveth son or daughter more than me is not worthy of me' (*Matt.* 10:37). To still this divine warning I put aside my Bible and began to work harder than ever. I recalled the vows made in seminary, and particularly on the day of my ordination: to be one of the best priests. This gave me a relative peace of mind for a few years.

The Sword of the Word of God

In January 1955, I had a pleasant surprise. Joseph Zacchello, the editor of the *Convert Magazine*, came to visit me while he was in Kansas City, Missouri. I was startled when he asked me if I was saved. This question haunted me and I prayed to God again to show me the way of salvation. It seemed to me that the voice of the Lord came clearly and reproachfully to me: 'Think not that I am come to send peace on earth: I came not to send peace, but a sword' (*Matt.* 10:34). That sword I used to cut myself off from everybody near and dear to me.

Today, having believed on the Lord for myself, I am experiencing how right he was when he said: 'There is no man that hath left house, or parents, or brethren, or wife, or children, for the kingdom of God's sake, who shall not receive manifold more in this present time, and in the world to come life everlasting' (*Luke* 18:29–30).

9

Benigno Zuniga:
Transformed by Christ

For more than fifty years I lived in complete spiritual darkness. Despite having been a priest for many years, my knowledge about Jesus Christ was very limited and distorted. In fact, for me, the real Christ of the Bible had been hidden under a blanket of complex religious teaching.

I believed that outside the Roman Catholic Church there was no possibility of salvation, and that the Pope, as Christ's representative on earth, was infallible. My loyalty was so great that I would have been willing to give my life in defence of the Pope.

The Teaching of the Church

I had been educated by Jesuit Fathers and decided to become a Jesuit monk at the age of sixteen. I studied in Peru, Ecuador, Spain, and Belgium and was later ordained a priest. For many years I taught in Catholic schools, held a position as a professor in a seminary, served as Vice-Chancellor of the Ecclesiastical Tribunal in my diocese, held the office of a chaplain in the army and served as a priest of two of the principal parishes of my country.

As a parish priest I set myself to opposing the Protestants in my area. I treated them as heretics, and I taught my people that they all held the lowest possible moral standards. As some of these Protestants continually appealed to the authority of the Bible, I decided to write a book exposing their error in the light of the Bible.

The Teaching of God

As I studied the Bible chapter by chapter over a period of three years, it came as a terrible shock to me to discover that I was the one in error. Far from being able to refute these heretics I found myself being refuted by my own Roman Catholic Bible. I began to see how far away from the Bible my Catholic beliefs were. Often as I studied I found myself moved to tears to think that I had submissively followed human ideas rather than the teaching of God.

Another effect of reading the Bible chapter by chapter was that I found my conscience come to life within me. I saw that I was personally a long way from God. As a priest I projected an image of holiness, but in reality I gave way to all kinds of sin and lived a thoroughly worldly life. The black robes which I wore symbolized the darkness of my heart. No amount of sacrament, prayer to the saints, penitence, holy water, or confession of sin to a human confessor could give me the peace that my soul began to long for.

Transformed by Christ

One day, although a priest over fifty years of age, I at last surrendered my heart to God. I knelt before Christ who, though invisible, became real and living to me. Feeling like a nobody, and with sorrow in my heart, I repented of having offended him by my awful life of sin. In my imagination, I saw the cross where his precious blood was shed to save me from the punishment I so richly deserved. The result of this prayer was that Christ transformed my life. He called me out of the tomb of spiritual darkness and brought me into a living experience and knowledge of himself.

The secret of true spiritual reality is to have a personal meeting with Christ through a sincere and vibrant faith. When Christ takes over a heart, every other spiritual blessing is assured. In the Scripture, salvation is seen clearly to be in him alone. For example the apostle Paul's ambition was, 'that I may win Christ and be found in him, not having mine own righteousness, which is of the law, but that which is through the faith of Christ, the righteousness which is of God by faith' (*Phil.* 3:8–9). In a similar way in the apostle John's writings, eternal life is in Christ and is found by believing on him: 'And we know that the Son of God is come, and hath given us an understanding, that we may know him that is true, and we are in him that is true, even in his Son Jesus Christ. This is the true God, and eternal life' (*1 John* 5:20).

BANNER *of* **TRUTH**

The Banner of Truth Trust originated in 1957 in London. The founders believed that much of the best literature of historic Christianity had been allowed to fall into oblivion and that, under God, its recovery could well lead not only to a strengthening of the church, but to true revival.

Interdenominational in vision, this publishing work is now international, and our lists include a number of contemporary authors, together with classics from the past. The translation of these books into many languages is encouraged.

A monthly magazine, *The Banner of Truth*, is also published, and further information about this, and all our other publications, may be found on our website, banneroftruth.org, or by contacting the offices below:

> *Head Office:*
> 3 Murrayfield Road
> Edinburgh
> EH12 6EL
> United Kingdom
> Email: info@banneroftruth.co.uk

> *North America Office:*
> PO Box 621
> Carlisle, PA 17013
> United States of America
> Email: info@banneroftruth.org